SCOTTISH CLASS

Volume Two

After a five year stronghold working passenger and freight trains on the West Highland and Far North lin
gradually replaced by the new sub-class of 37/4. Initially 25 Class 37/4s were allocated to Eastfield, 17 stayed while eight moved to Inverness. Although a number of 37/0s remained at each depot, their steam heat boilers became obsolete, making them essentially freight-only machines although occasionally, in the summer months, they still worked passenger trains.

Due to the introduction of the 37/4s, many of the former Scottish celebrities like 37012 'Loch Rannoch' and 37043 'Loch Lomond' were transferred away. Some were renumbered, others were rebuilt and in time all of them lost their Scottish identities. Although the class of 1980-1985 was disbanded, the new 37/4s took over their former identities and names and these once faceless, virtually unknown South Wales-based locos became Scottish celebrities in their own right. 37408 became the new 'Loch Rannoch' and 37412 was 'Loch Lomond' to name just two. Finished in the attractive bright Large Logo blue livery, the new sub-class got to work on West Highland and Far North trains. Within a couple of years, these locos dominated everything and things look set to continue that way for many years.

By the late 1980s, as British Rail geared itself up for privatisation, the Scottish scene changed too. The once proud loco-hauled trains were replaced by Sprinter DMUs with their cramped carriages and lack of luggage space. It was the end of these attractive and popular trains, with their comfortable compartment carriages, and the whole ambience of rail travel in Scotland changed too. The traditional carriage of mail, parcels and newspapers was lost to road, ending an era dating right back to the opening of the railways. The 37/4s were repainted into odd liveries, some were transferred away and all of them were placed into operating pools. Then in 1992, Eastfield depot closed, bringing another huge chapter in Scottish rail history to a close. There was of course a further twist to the tale when the loco-hauled trains made a mini comeback in the early 1990s and 37/0s replaced the 37/4s, but that's another story!

Welcome to my second book on Scottish Class 37s. For this volume I've tried to keep the photos to the 1985-1990 period when 37/0s and 37/4s were painted in the BR Blue or BR Large Logo liveries. During this period a lot of new liveries appeared but I've decided to keep this collection true blue, saving the multi-coloured styles for a third volume.

Once again I am greatly in debt to the people who have made this book possible. I would like to thank Bill Watson for his superb landscape images. I was so pleased to be able to use these I decided to give each slide a full page to itself, without cropping or the addition of text. The captions are on the opposite or previous page. I hope you don't mind flicking back or forward to read the caption. I would like to thank Jim Ramsay for his help with the text and for identifying various locations. A couple of slides in this book came with no information and thanks to Jim, who recognised features like mountains or station buildings, I was able to write about them. Thanks to Peter D Scott, Peter Scott, Ken White and John Watterson for their slides and photos. Thanks to everybody at WP Litho for their professionalism. Thanks also to Mary, Elizabeth and Jason. Without your help none of this would be possible.

Enjoy the book

Nick Meskell

September 2005

First Published 2005
ISBN 0-9548035-4-X

Train Crazy *Publishing*

Printed by WP Litho of Wiltshire

EASTFIELD LOCOS

The 37/0s

In Volume One we looked at the loco allocation for Eastfield in 1982, 1984 and 1986. To set the theme for this book, I've stepped back to the start of 1985 to show which 37/0s were based at this depot prior to the introduction of the 37/4s. The table below shows the full allocation from January 1985 and what happened next to each locomotive.

37 011	Air and vacuum brakes	Steam heat boiler	Withdrawn, August 1987
37 012	Air and vacuum brakes	Steam heat boiler	Transferred to Motherwell, October 1987
37 014	Air and vacuum brakes	Steam heat boiler	Transferred to Motherwell, October 1987
37 017	Vacuum brakes	Steam heat boiler	Transferred to Cardiff, August 1985
37 018	Air and vacuum brakes	No train heat	Transferred to Stratford, May 1985
37 022	Air and vacuum brakes	Steam heat boiler	Transferred to Thornaby, August 1986
37 026	Air and vacuum brakes	Steam heat boiler	Transferred to Motherwell, April 1986
37 027	Air and vacuum brakes	Steam heat boiler	Transferred to Thornaby, March 1987
37 033	Air and vacuum brakes	Steam heat boiler	Transferred to Motherwell, March 1988
37 037	Air and vacuum brakes	Steam heat boiler	Transferred to Motherwell, December 1985
37 039	Air and vacuum brakes	Steam heat boiler	Transferred to Cardiff, September 1985
37 043	Air and vacuum brakes	Steam heat boiler	Transferred to Stratford, October 1987
37 051	Air and vacuum brakes	Steam heat boiler	Transferred to Motherwell, May 1987
37 081	Air and vacuum brakes	Steam heat boiler	Transferred to Cardiff, May 1986
37 085	Air and vacuum brakes	Steam heat boiler	Transferred to Cardiff, March 1988
37 090	Vacuum brakes	Steam heat boiler	Transferred to Cardiff, January 1986
37 108	Air and vacuum brakes	Steam heat boiler	Transferred to Motherwell, April 1986
37 111	Air and vacuum brakes	Steam heat boiler	Transferred to Motherwell, January 1986
37 112	Air and vacuum brakes	Steam heat boiler	Transferred to Cardiff, February 1986
37 124	Air and vacuum brakes	No train heat	Transferred to Landore, March 1985
37 144	Air and vacuum brakes	No train heat	Transferred to March, May 1985
37 147	Air and vacuum brakes	No train heat	Transferred to Landore, March 1985
37 148	Air and vacuum brakes	No train heat	Transferred to Motherwell, March 1985
37 149	Air and vacuum brakes	No train heat	Transferred to Landore, March 1985
37 157	Air and vacuum brakes	No train heat	Transferred to Cardiff, February 1986
37 171	Air and vacuum brakes	No train heat	Transferred to Cardiff, March 1985
37 172	Air and vacuum brakes	No train heat	Transferred to Cardiff, March 1985
37 175	Air and vacuum brakes	Steam heat boiler	Transferred to Laira, May 1986
37 178	Air and vacuum brakes	Steam heat boiler	Transferred to Stratford, November 1987
37 179	Air and vacuum brakes	Steam heat boiler isolated	Transferred to Cardiff, March 1985
37 184	Air and vacuum brakes	Steam heat boiler	Transferred to Motherwell, December 1985
37 188	Air and vacuum brakes	Steam heat boiler	Transferred to Motherwell, December 1985
37 190	Air and vacuum brakes	Steam heat boiler	Transferred to Motherwell, October 1985
37 191	Air and vacuum brakes	Steam heat boiler	Transferred to Cardiff, September 1990
37 192	Air and vacuum brakes	Steam heat boiler	Transferred to Cardiff, March 1985
37 237	Air and vacuum brakes	No train heat	Transferred to Landore, March 1985
37 253	Vacuum brakes	No train heat	Transferred to Cardiff, March 1985
37 265	Air and vacuum brakes	Steam heat boiler isolated	Transferred to Motherwell, May 1985

The 37/4s

To replace the eight steam heat locos, eight former South Wales 37/0s passed through Crewe Works and emerged as 37 414 to 37 421. Unlike the Eastfield locos, none of the previous names carried by the 37/0s were transferred to the 37/4s. Sadly, wonderful names like 'Dunrobin Castle' (37 114), 'Caithness' (37 261) and 'Dounreay' (37 262) were lost forever. The table below shows the early history of the Inverness based 37/4s.

Old No.	Prev. Depot	New No.	Named
37 268	Cardiff	37 401	Mary Queen of Scots on 4th November 1985 at Linlithgow station
37 274	Cardiff	37 402	Oor Wullie on 14th December 1985 at Glasgow Queen Street station
37 307	Landore	37 403	Isle of Mull on 3rd January 1986 at Oban station
37 286	Cardiff	37 404	Ben Cruachan on 3rd January 1986 at Oban station
37 282	Cardiff	37 405	Strathclyde Region on 11th April 1986 at Glasgow Queen Street station
37 295	Cardiff	37 406	The Saltaire Society on 28th June 1986 at Eastfield TMD
37 305	Landore	37 407	Loch Long on 28th June 1986 at Eastfield TMD
37 289	Cardiff	37 408	Loch Rannoch on 1st September 1986 at Eastfield TMD
37 270	Cardiff	37 409	Loch Awe on 27th August 1986 at Eastfield TMD
37 273	Cardiff	37 410	Aluminium 100 on 21st September 1986 at Lynemouth, Alcan Works
37 290	Cardiff	37 411	The Institution of Railway Signal Engineers on 28th May 1987 at Fort William station
37 301	Landore	37 412	Loch Lomond on 10th March 1987 at Eastfield TMD
37 276	Cardiff	37 413	Loch Eil Outward Bound on 1st March 1987 at Eastfield TMD
37 266	Landore	37 422	(no name)
37 296	Landore	37 423	Sir Murray Morrison 1873 - 1948. Pioneer of the British Aluminium Industry on 18th May 1988 at Fort William station
37 279	Cardiff	37 424	Glendarroch on 9th December 1987 at Glasgow Queen Street station
37 292	Cardiff	37 425	Sir Robert McAlpine (one side) on 14th October 1986 at Fort William station Concrete Bob (one side) on 14th October 1986 at Glenfinnian station

Front cover: The traditional photograph at Oban station with 37 401 'Mary Queen of Scots' on 2nd April 1988. With at least two Mark 2 coaches in tow, the train loads prior to departing as 1T28, the 13.00 to Glasgow Queen Street. Starting life based at Sheffield, D6968 latterly 37 268 moved to Stratford in November 1967 and then Cardiff a decade later. Following conversion to a 37/4, this loco led a fascinating life, based at Eastfield, Motherwell, Cardiff, Crewe and Toton and today, it is still a regular performer on the West Highland line, painted in Royal Scotsman livery. Completed in 1902, McCaig's Tower overlooks the ever changing railway scene. *(Peter Scott)*

Inside front cover: In perfect lighting conditions, 37 188 'Jimmy Shand' pulls away from Bridge of Orchy with 1T34, the 14.15 Fort William to Glasgow Queen Street on 30th July 1985. Note the semaphore signals. This loco was named at Oban station on 10th May 1985. Although the livery 'Large Logo' was the general term, there were a few variations over the years. 37 188 was one of 16 Eastfield locos which received a grey roof as opposed to black. Other grey examples were: 37 011, 37 021, 37 025, 37 027, 37 035, 37 043, 37 081, 37 111, 37 114, 37 183, 37 191, 37 260, 37 261, 37 262 and 37 264. *(Bill Watson)*

Photo page 6: The introduction of Mark 3 sleeper coaches on the Euston - Fort William services brought regular air braked passenger trains to the West Highlands for the first time in October 1983. With steam heat 37/0s unable to provide the necessary Electric Train Supply (ETS), three redundant Class 25s were converted at Aberdeen into mobile ETS locos. All three were painted in a blue/grey livery and received a peculiar white Highland terrier logo with a red background! 37 085 with 97 251 (aka ETHEL 2 and formerly 25 305) leave Crianlarich for the climb to Tyndrum Upper on 11th May 1985 working 1S07, the 21.00 London Euston to Fort William. *(Bill Watson)*

Photo page 7: The additional weight of an ETHEL plus the Mark 3 stock often proved troublesome for a single Class 37 during poor railhead conditions. To combat this, on Mondays only, mostly during the autumn and winter, a Class 20 was used to provide additional power, working in multiple with the 37 and giving what was almost a Class 37/20/25 triple-header! 20 045 and 20 085 were fitted with a through steam pipe for this working. In the morning mist of 18th June 1985, 37 191 'International Youth Year 1985' appears to be coping perfectly well on its own with 97 250 (ETHEL 1 / 25 310) and 1S07 as they pass Inverhaggernie Farm Crossing. *(Bill Watson)*

Opposite: 37 192 at Mallaig on 6th July 1985 ready to depart with 1Y54, the 12.20 to Fort William. There is something exceptionally pleasing about a BR blue Class 37 with a black headcode box and a rake of blue and grey Mark 1s in tow. At this time there was a mixture of open and compartment stock operating on the West Highland lines. On this particular train, the rear coach is a BSK with the last compartment (and toilet area), converted to a buffet counter. *(Peter D Scott)*

Above: Having travelled behind 37 192 from Mallaig, the photographer took this image of two 37s together at Fort William. Without a headlight, 37 049 stands to the left, loading 1T34, the 14.15 to Glasgow Queen Street, while 37 192 has run around its train and will be first out with 2Y53, the 14.05 back to Mallaig. Remarkably, both these locos have circular buffers. The majority of other Eastfield-based locos in this book (and Volume One) have oval buffers. *(Peter D Scott)*

Photo page 10: The practice of double-heading on the West Highland lines was common throughout the 1980s. Not only was it an opportunity to balance loco positions (and avoid unnecessary light engine moves on a single line railway), certain trains required the extra power. In the photo, perhaps two locos weren't needed here but nevertheless they make a fine sight. Pictured on the approach to Bridge of Orchy, 37 026 'Loch Awe' and 37 190 power 7D10, the 06.05 from Fort William to Mossend on 20th June 1985. *(Bill Watson)*

Photo page 11: A friendly wave from the driver greets the cameraman as 37 108 and 37 184 exit the Horseshoe Curve near Tyndrum Summit on 30th May 1985 with 7D10. With both locos taking power, it's almost possible to hear that thunderous English Electric roar echoing off the surrounding mountains. *(Bill Watson)*

Opposite: Towards the end of their days at Eastfield, many of the former boilered examples were relegated to freight duties which took them away from their original haunts. Pictured at Carlisle on 5th July 1990, a somewhat weather-beaten and scruffy 37 191 waits at a red signal. Having had its nameplates removed in November 1985 (ten months after they were fitted!), 37 191 ended its association with Scotland with a move to Cardiff in October 1990. Nine years later the loco was withdrawn and in January 2001 it was scrapped. *(John Watterson)*

Above: Although most photos of the Eastfield based locos in this book are taken on the scenic West Highland lines, it should be remembered that they could also be found on passenger and freight trains in other parts of Scotland. One of the lesser known Eastfield type 3s, 37 170 is pictured here on a unorthodox two coach train on 17th September 1990. Deputising for a failed or unavailable DMU, the 18.08 Montrose to Perth calls at Carnoustie. Note the carriages: a former BCK (now declassified) and an Inter City liveried Mark 1 TSO. (Note to train companies: This is what a two coach train should look like!). *(Nick Meskell collection)*

Above: In the beginning: 37 268 at Crewe Works in April or May of 1985 undergoing overhaul and conversion to become the very first ETS-fitted Class 37. Note the chalked number underneath the first grill on the bonnet '268 to 401'. In addition to the new front end cables, a centre headlight has been fitted under the route indicator box. Although fitted with headlights in various positions over the years, working off Inverness and Eastfield, this central position became standard for Class 37s during future overhauls. The all new 37 401 worked the test train from Crewe to Llandudno Junction and back on 19th June 1985 hauling nine coaches. *(Ken White)*

Opposite: And here is the finished beast, complete with a large dog logo, black headcode boxes and nameplates. (This is the same end as in the photo opposite). After a few ECS moves and test runs around Eastfield, 37 401 (with 37 403) worked their first passenger train in Scotland on Wednesday 3rd July 1985, 1L33, the 11.05 Glasgow Queen Street to Perth. Although probably not required anyway, the locos were unable to heat the stock as coach SC4749 (a Mark 1 TSO) at the head of the train, was steam-heat only! (Progress indeed!). In the photo, 37 401 slows for the station stop at Tyndrum Lower working 1Y13, the 12.20 Glasgow Queen Street to Oban on 1st March 1986. *(Bill Watson)*

Opposite: 37 407 calls at Crianlarich on 9th August 1986 working 1Y21, the 09.50 from Glasgow Queen Street to Fort William. At this time, the loco was just over a year old and retained a yellow headcode box with hand painted fleet numbers. Upon arrival at Fort William, 37 407 worked the 16.05 to Mallaig, then the 18.50 back to Fort William, finishing with the 21.05 back to Mallaig, arriving at 22.35. This was a total passenger mileage of 247 which was fairly typical for a 37/4 at this time. In turn, the loco worked the first train from Mallaig (06.05 to Fort William) the following day.
(Nick Meskell collection)

Above: Absolutely brand new, 37 405 stands at Eastfield in 1985, prior to being named and without miniature snowploughs. Originally there were plans to name this loco 'Eastfield' but instead, it became 'Strathclyde Region'. Following a collision with a Class 156 DMU at Craigendorran in April 1991, the loco suffered severe damage to both cabs and was stored unserviceable for a while. Thankfully the repairs took place and the loco went on to work for many years, based at Motherwell, Tinsley, Immingham, Crewe, Stratford, Toton and Cardiff. Remarkably, at the time of writing, the loco is still going strong and now based at Margam, it worked 2F05, the 07.17 Rhymney to Cardiff on 9th August 2005. *(Peter Scott collection)*

Photo page 18: These two images beautifully sum up the winter wonderland appearance of the West Highland line. 37 402 'Oor Wullie' approaches Bridge of Orchy on 14th April 1986 with the first southbound passenger train of the day, 1T18, the 08.40 from Fort William to Glasgow Queen Street. Obviously only three coaches were needed on this cold Monday morning, two weeks after Easter. That was always the beauty of loco-hauled trains on the West Highland line, if the passengers were there, extra coaches could easily be added, without the need of additional engines, loco crews or relief trains. *(Bill Watson)*

Photo page 19: Taken six weeks earlier, on 1st March, 37 403 'Isle of Mull' passes Achaladder Farm, just after Bridge of Orchy, working 1Y21, the 09.50 from Glasgow Queen Street to Fort William. For the photographer it must have been a sensational sight and sound to witness a 37 on full power in such a dramatic landscape and in such perfect lighting conditions. Surely one of the joys of life for any Class 37 fan! *(Bill Watson)*

Opposite: It would be easy to compile a book of locos in perfect sunny weather but that wouldn't truly depict the West Highland line. Anybody who has been to Scotland will know that bright sunshine is often hard to come by and even on fine days, perfect weather can be spoiled by the odd shower. Sunshine after the rain with 37 404 'Ben Cruachan' at Crianlarich on 2nd April 1988 working 1T18, the 08.30 from Fort William to Glasgow Queen Street. *(Peter Scott)*

Above: Crianlarich station at 16.35 on Thursday 18th August 1988 and two raincoat clad figures await the arrival of 1T34, the 14.45 from Fort William to Glasgow Queen Street. Bursting out of the late afternoon mist, 37 406 leads its train into the station. Note the front end damage to the loco and the unusual crooked numbers! (Was this to disguise the dent?). First coach behind the loco is a former BCK. The toilet and first compartment are now a buffet counter. The fifth and sixth full windows were the former first class compartments. *(Nick Meskell collection)*

Above: 37 425 'Sir Robert McAlpine/Concrete Bob' at Glasgow Queen Street on 18th October 1986, about to depart with 1Y23, the 16.50 to Fort William. 'Bob' was only six months old at the time. This was one of Eastfield's longest diagrams which started with the 06.50 from Mallaig to Fort William, then the 08.40 to Glasgow Queen Street, returning to Fort William on this train. On this particular day, 37 425 failed at Rhu, just north of Helensburgh Upper, 27 miles out of Glasgow. Assistance came from Eastfield stablemate 37 404 which worked the train through to Fort William.
(Nick Meskell collection)

Opposite: A superb summer morning scene on the Fort William line with 37 408 'Loch Rannoch' running down from Tyndrum Summit on 5th August 1987. It's a very traditional railway scene with bullhead rail on wooden sleepers, an interesting mixture of wagons, a brightly painted named locomotive and a dramatic landscape of mountains and forests. The train is 7Y31, the 05.10 from Mossend to Fort William. *(Bill Watson)*

Above: An interesting viewpoint from Crianlarich with 37 424 departing on 1Y13, the 12.20 Glasgow Queen Street to Oban on 4th September 1987. The line on the left is the stub of the old Caley line which ran through to Crianlarich Lower, Killin and beyond. The line from Fort William can be glimpsed passing over the grey bridge in the distance. Despite only having worked for about 20 months since conversion, 37 424 clearly shows the perils of West Highland life at this time. As well as being filthy, the loco sports front end accident damage and a partial repaint in the wrong shade of yellow. 37 424 was named two months after this photo was taken. Hopefully it was repainted, or at least washed before then! *(Nick Meskell collection)*

Opposite: It would have been a sin to omit a slide as good as this so there are no apologies for another image of 37 401. 'Mary Queen of Scots' climbs past Inverhaggernie Farm after leaving Crianlarich on the 6S56, 07.12 Blyth Dock to Fort William Alcan hoppers on 10th May 1988. *(Bill Watson)*

Page 26 photo: Thunder in the mountains and it was nothing to do with the weather! A stunning image of 37 425 'Sir Robert McAlpine/Concrete Bob' taken on 14th June 1988 on the last stretch to Tyndrum Summit on 1D15, the 18.10 Fort William to Mossend Yard (which joined with a portion from Inverness and continued to Euston). Note the former BCK/buffet coach behind the loco and an Inter City liveried Mark 2 BSO third in. The split at Mossend would have seen the front two coaches stay behind for the morning leg back to Fort William while the remainder of the train would have run through to London. *(Bill Watson)*

INVERNESS LOCOS

The 37/0s

In the same format as the Eastfield locos, here is the Inverness allocation as of January 1985, the last full year prior to the introduction of the 37/4s and what happened next to each locomotive:

37 025	Air and vacuum brakes	Steam heat boiler	Transferred to Eastfield, January 1986
37 035	Air and vacuum brakes	Steam heat boiler	Transferred to Eastfield, January 1986
37 114	Air and vacuum brakes	Steam heat boiler	Transferred to Eastfield, May 1990
37 183	Air and vacuum brakes	Steam heat boiler	Transferred to Eastfield, January 1986
37 260	Air and vacuum brakes	Steam heat boiler	Withdrawn, August 1989
37 261	Air and vacuum brakes	Steam heat boiler	Transferred to Eastfield, May 1990
37 262	Air and vacuum brakes	Steam heat boiler	Transferred to Eastfield, May 1990
37 264	Air and vacuum brakes	Steam heat boiler	Transferred to Eastfield, January 1986

The 37/4s

To replace the eight steam heat locos, eight former South Wales 37/0s passed through Crewe Works and emerged as 37 414 to 37 421. Unlike the Eastfield locos, none of the previous names carried by the 37/0s were transferred to the 37/4s. Sadly, wonderful names like 'Dunrobin Castle' (37 114), 'Caithness' (37 261) and 'Dounreay' (37 262) were lost forever. The table below shows the early history of the Inverness based 37/4s.

Old No.	Prev. Depot	New No.	Named
37 287	Cardiff	37 414	(no name)
37 277	Cardiff	37 415	(no name)
37 302	Landore	37 416	(no name)
37 269	Cardiff	37 417	Highland Region on 16th December 1985 at Inverness station
37 271	Cardiff	37 418	An Comunn Gaidhealach on 10th October 1986 at Edinburgh station
37 291	Cardiff	37 419	(no name)
37 297	Cardiff	37 420	The Scottish Hosteller on 28th June 1986 at Inverness station
37 267	Landore	37 421	(no name)

Page 27 photo: The last of our Eastfield images shows 37 411 'The Institute of Railway Signal Engineers' leaving Horseshoe Curve and commencing the climb to Tyndrum Summit on 5th August 1987 working 7D10. *(Bill Watson)*

Opposite: The introduction of radio signalling on the Far North lines, marked by the naming of 37 260 'Radio Highland', meant the end of traditional semaphores and signal boxes. In this 6th May 1985 dated photo at Dingwall, the signal box stands silent and although the signal posts remain, the arms have gone. 37 114 still in standard BR blue and without nameplates, approaches the station with 2H82, the 11.10 from Kyle of Lochalsh to Inverness. Heading north and sporting the large logo livery is 37 025 on an SRPS excursion. *(Nick Meskell collection)*

Page 30 photo: A month after the photo on page 29, 37 114 was repainted into Large Logo livery and named 'Dunrobin Castle'. Working the same train as before, the very smart and attractive 37 114 skirts Loch a' Chuilinn on 29th July 1986. Note the black headcode boxes and the trailing load of eight Mark 1 coaches. *(Bill Watson)*

37 153 pauses at Aviemore in October 1988. Fresh from the paint shop (first day out?) the loco sports a revised version of the large logo livery which included black painted grills on the bonnet-side. Originally painted yellow, the area was prone to collecting dirt and proved difficult to wash. To avoid these problems, it was painted black! Allocated to Landore from new (in July 1963), this loco first moved to Scotland in August 1966, based at Polmadie. After a spell at Haymarket, the loco moved to Eastfield in March 1972. While many Eastern Region Class 37s moved north in the early 1980s, 37 153 moved in the opposite direction and began working off Immingham from July 1981. In July 1988, the loco was transferred to Inverness for the first time and enjoyed spells at Eastfield and Motherwell until 1999. The loco was scrapped in January 2003. Other than the number change from D6853 to 37 153 (in 1974), this loco was never again renumbered, nor was it ever named. This was quite unusual for a machine with such a rich Scottish history. *(Nick Meskell collection)*

Above: Crew change at Ardgay on Sunday 7th July 1985 with 37 264 heading south on 2H64, the 14.50 from Wick to Inverness. Note the oil tail lamp of the northbound service. In between two spells at Eastfield, 37 264 worked off Inverness depot between October 1984 and January 1986. Withdrawn in 1999, the loco is one of a number of former Scottish-based Class 37s to make it into preservation and is currently undergoing restoration at the Birmingham Railway Museum in Tyseley. *(Peter D Scott)*

Below: Further to the point about black bonnet-side grills, 37 262 'Dounreay' is a prime example of how dirty these became. The loco is pictured on Inverness depot on 21st June 1986 with 37 155 of Motherwell depot behind. 1986 was the first full summer of 37/4s on the Far North lines, which must have drastically reduced the operating mileage of the surviving 37/0s. Having said that, records from June 1986, show that 37 262 was the Georgemas Junction - Thurso loco for three days between the 9th and the 11th, before a move back to Inverness on the 12th and on the last day of the month, the loco worked the 06.00 from Wick to Inverness having worked up to Wick the evening before.
(Nick Meskell collection)

Opposite: The barren Highland landscape with its numerous lochs, rivers and streams heading north west from Lochluichart (36 miles out of Inverness) towards the Kyle of Lochalsh makes this 82 mile railway one of the most scenic in the British Isles. What better way to see it all than from the window of a Mark 1 coach hauled by a British built type 3 locomotive? 37 414 crosses Loch a' Chuilinn viaduct working 2H81, the 06.55 from Inverness to Kyle of Lochalsh on 30th July 1986. *(Bill Watson)*

Above: 37 418 'An Comunn Gaidhealach' propels its carriages into Inverness station on 6th September 1987 prior to working 2H65, the 16.05 (Sundays only) to Wick. Spread over a weekend, this was a three-day out and back diagram from Inverness which started on the Saturday with the 06.55 to Kyle, 11.30 to Inverness then the 17.35 to Wick. On the Sunday the loco worked the 11.20 Wick to Inverness, returning on the 16.05 to Wick. The Monday started with the 06.00 Wick to Inverness, 11.35 back to Wick and finally, the 18.00 Wick to Inverness. Although there were opportunities to swap the loco at Inverness, unless it was faulty or due an exam, there is no reason why it wouldn't have completed the full three days, clocking a hefty 1,134 passenger miles! *(Nick Meskell collection)*

Above: An unidentified location (guesses are Dingwall or Muir of Ord?) with 37 415 heading north on 22nd April 1989. The train consist of a full brake as the second coach would mean a Kyle train although a BSK as coach four means two brake sections, resulting in a perfect split for Georgemas Junction. Whatever the train, 37 415 was one of a few 37/4s which worked on a passenger train instead of a designated test train from Crewe upon completion of overhaul. On 30th October 1985, 37 415 topped 33 057 on 1D27, the 11.15 from Crewe to Bangor. After running round at Bangor, the same pair returned on 1V06, the 14.17 from Bangor to Cardiff with the 37 being detached at Crewe. It would seem that all was not well with 37 415 as it worked a further designated test train to Llandudno Junction on 12th November and then 1D27/1V06 (this time with 33 042) on 27th November. The loco was working off Inverness by January 1986. *(Nick Meskell collection)*

Below: One of the most delightful aspects of operation on the Far North lines was the splitting (and joining) of trains at Georgemas Junction. At this location, the loco which had worked from Inverness would take two or three coaches forward to Wick while a second loco stabled at Georgemas Junction would take the other two or three coaches forward to Thurso. After running round their respective trains at Wick and Thurso, both locos returned to Georgemas Junction, the carriages were recoupled and the Wick loco took the whole train forward to Inverness. The loco from Thurso then waited four or five hours for the next Inverness arrival and the process was repeated. On 27th April 1988, 37 420 'The Scottish Hosteller' stands at the top of the two coach portion for Thurso (2H72), with 37 417 'Highland Region' at the other end of the station ready for Wick - having worked in from Inverness (2H63, 11.35 departure). Note the perfect cloudless sky - very rare! *(Peter Scott)*

Opposite: Pictured at Thurso running around its two coach train (from the previous page) 37 420 'The Scottish Hosteller' looks awesome in the perfect spring sunshine. For the record, the Merseyside-based photographer logged the following move to get to Thurso: 26th April 1988: 304 034 - 21.50 Liverpool Lime Street to Crewe; 87 030 - 23.14 Crewe to Mossend Yard. 27th April 1988: 47 633 - 04.45 Mossend Yard to Inverness; 08 754 - Stock backshunt at Inverness; 37 417 - 11.35 Inverness to Georgemas Junction; 37 420 - 15.34 Georgemas Junction to Thurso; 37 420 - 18.02 Thurso to Georgemas Junction; 37 417 - 18.27 Georgemas Junction to Inverness and 47 604 - 23.40 Inverness to Glasgow Queen Street. Talk about dedication and lack of sleep! Fantastic! *(Peter Scott)*

Above: The ultimate in Scottish rail travel in the late 1980s: one loco and two coaches! 37 417 stands at Wick on 20th November 1987 prior to departure with 2H62, the 12.00 to Inverness. Evidently, passengers are in short supply on this sunny but cold late-autumn Friday morning. When it comes to railway coach design, none could beat the Mark 1 BCK (behind the loco). With space for luggage, parcels and mail, a guard's area, two first class compartments (12 seats), three second class compartments (18 seats) and a toilet, the BCK really could offer everything! 37 417 was the first Class 37/4 to work a passenger train north from Inverness. On 8th January 1986, the loco worked 2H83, the 10.55 to Kyle of Lochalsh. Later the same day 37 418 made its Highland debut with 2H85, the 17.55 to Kyle. *(Peter Scott)*

Above: The steel grey sky sets the mood for this image of 37 421 at Wick on 22nd April 1989. The daffodils to the right can't hide the menace in the background - an unnumbered Class 156 DMU. Just over three years earlier, on 14th January 1986, 37 421 opened its Highland account working 2H61, the 06.35 from Inverness to Wick. This loco was marooned north of Inverness when the River Ness bridge collapsed on 7th February 1989. Although locos and stock were moved back and forth by road, a temporary depot was set up at Muir of Ord (MO). Official records from January 1990, show 37 418, 37 419 and 37 420 based at MO. Five Class 156s (sets 156 446, 457, 474, 477 and 478) were also moved by road and outbased at MO. Muir of Ord station was closed to passengers at this time, with a replacement bus running between Inverness and Dingwall, calling at Muir of Ord. Train services ran north from Dingwall until the new rail bridge across the River Ness was opened in May 1990. One final point to make is that 37 421 was reallocated to Laira in January 1989 but got trapped! In 1990 it moved to Eastfield and then Immingham. *(Nick Meskell collection)*

Below: The weather-beaten 37 419 stands at Kyle of Lochalsh on 4th October 1988 prior to working the last train of the day to Inverness, 2H84, the 16.40 departure. During the winter timetable of 1988/89, there were three trains a day from Kyle to Inverness, departing at 07.10, 11.28 and 16.40 - Mondays to Saturdays. There was no Sunday service. The three coach rake was typical for this line at this time with the full brake vehicle in the middle (or second behind the loco). 37 419 boasts unusual front end numbers and the blue BR totem sticker reads 'THURSO'. This loco ended its first association with Scotland in January 1991 with a move to Thornaby. Later depots included Tinsley, Immingham, Springs Branch, Crewe and Cardiff; working commuter trains between Manchester Victoria and Southport and then hundreds, maybe thousands of journeys on the 23 mile long Cardiff - Rhymney circuit. *(Peter Scott)*

Above: Gleaming in the summer sunshine at Kyle of Lochalsh, 37 416, fresh from the paint shop and without miniature snowploughs, draws forward from its carriages having worked the 11.10 from Inverness on 21st July 1987. Considering the loco was only about 21 months out of Crewe at this time, it must have been quite shabby to warrant a full repaint. This particular train was a summer-only affair which included a former 1958-built Class 101 trailer car No.M54356 as an observation coach on the rear (for which supplement fares were charged). *(Nick Meskell collection)*

Opposite: Having run around its train (opposite) 37 416 was sent to the sidings to shunt a couple of ballast hoppers before departing with the 15.50 back to Inverness. This was one of the great features of loco-hauled trains, sadly missing from today's railways. Not only could 37 416 bring up a full brake van of mail or parcels, hundreds of rucksacks or cases, two dozen bicycles, a dozen surf boards, oil and chemicals, car parts, livestock or even a box of supplies for the station toilets, the loco (maybe with the same crew) could shunt a couple of wagons, perhaps marshal a train or even work a short journey to the next yard and after all this, that same loco would depart with the service train and take its passengers in comfort back south. One loco - one train - hundreds of uses. How do you get two dozen bicycles on a modern two-car DMU? *(Nick Meskell collection)*

MOTHERWELL LOCOS

Originally it was intended that only Eastfield and Inverness based locos should feature in this book, but it is important to mention the small pool of Class 37/0s cascaded from the 37/4 programme which in 1986 were renumbered and based at Motherwell for air braked Scottish steel traffic. Among them were a few former Eastfield favourites including 37 026 'Loch Awe', 37 037, 37 049, 37 108, 37 111 'Loch Eil Outward Bound' and 37 190. All these locos had their vacuum brakes isolated and of those which still had them, their steam heat boilers were also isolated. All previous names were removed. The table below shows the situation:

Old No.	New No.	Date	Named
37 152	37 310	February 1986	British Steel Ravenscraig on 4th March 1986 at Motherwell Station
37 156	37 311	March 1986	British Steel Hunterson on 4th March 1986 at Motherwell Station
37 137	37 312	July 1986	Clyde Iron on 24th July 1986 at Motherwell TMD
37 145	37 313	August 1986	(no name)
37 190	37 314	July 1986	Dalzell on 25th July 1986 at Motherwell TMD
37 026	37 320	July 1986	Shap Fell on 23rd July 1986 at Motherwell TMD
37 037	37 321	July 1986	Gartcosh on 23rd July 1986 at Motherwell TMD
37 049	37 322	July 1986	Imperial on 24th July 1986 at Motherwell TMD
37 088	37 323	July 1986	Clydesdale on 23rd July 1986 at Motherwell TMD
37 099	37 324	July 1986	Clydebridge on 27th July 1986 at Motherwell TMD
37 108	37 325	August 1986	Lanarkshire Steel on 6th August 1986 at Motherwell TMD
37 111	37 326	July 1986	Glengarnock on 23rd July 1986 at Motherwell TMD

Undated, but probably a Sunday in 1987 and 37 323 'Clydesdale' leads a fantastic line-up of six split-headcode Class 37s on Motherwell depot.
(Nick Meskell collection)

Also at Motherwell, 37 322 'Imperial' awaits its next turn of duty. With the large bodyside number and Motherwell depot 'salmon' motif, this was a kind of a pseudo-Large Logo livery but without the huge BR symbol and yellow cab ends. Close inspection of the front end, reveals the former vacuum brake pipe still in situ while the steam heat pipe has been removed. *(Nick Meskell collection)*

Above: Absolutely filthy, but absolutely gorgeous, 37 313 with 37 047 at Carstairs Junction on 7th October 1988. The late 1980s were very much a transitional period not only for liveries, renumbering and operating pools, but also for loco fixtures and fittings. The 37/4s with their centre headlights, miniature snowploughs and subsequent orange cantrail stripes were the new order while the external appearance of locos like 37 313 here were barely altered from the 1970s. Of the dozen dedicated locos in this (FMGM) Motherwell-based pool, 37 313 was the only unnamed one. 37 047 was Stratford-based at the time of this photo, operating in the LXXA pool (Freightliner Traffic General). *(Nick Meskell collection)*

Below: In 1989 it was all over. The 12 locos were simply renumbered back to their old 37/0 identities and in time their vacuum train brakes were reinstated. Still based at Motherwell, eventually they were moved far and wide although the majority kept their nameplates for a number of years. 37 108 'Lanarkshire Steel', with its panelled over bonnet doors, stayed at Motherwell until a move to Stratford in June 1991. Today 37 108 is owned by Type 3 Traction and is undergoing restoration at Carnforth. *(Nick Meskell collection)*

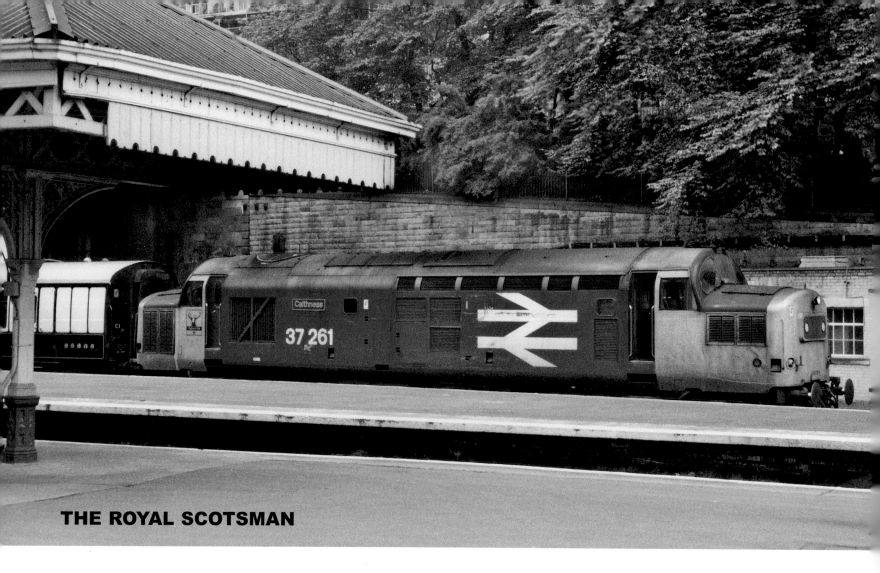

THE ROYAL SCOTSMAN

Above: The introduction of Class 37/4s in Scotland led to the demise of the Class 37/0s on passenger trains, however the introduction of the Royal Scotsman luxury train provided salvation for a few engines. Essentially aimed at American visitors, for £2,200 (per person in 1985) the passenger enjoyed a seven day Class 37 haulage extravaganza around some of Scotland's finest attractions. Four Inverness-based 37/0s were given the task of hauling this train plus any other land cruise or special which required Class 37 power in northern Scotland. In the case of the Royal Scotsman, the same loco often stuck with the train for the entire week. Over the years the travel itinerary has varied immensely but in the summer of 1985, this was the week-long programme: Wednesday - Edinburgh to Oban; Thursday - Oban to Fort William; Friday - Fort William to Mallaig (Steam), Mallaig to Fort William (Steam), then Fort William to Ladybank; Saturday - Ladybank to Edinburgh then Keith; Sunday - Keith to Kyle, Kyle to Keith; Monday - Keith to Dunrobin Castle, Dunrobin Castle to Boat of Garten; Tuesday - Boat of Garten to Edinburgh. In the photo, 37 261 'Caithness' prepares to set sail from Edinburgh on 4th April 1987. Quite remarkably, after reallocation, withdrawal, a spell working in France, parts removal, no hope and no future, 37 261 was privately purchased in 2001, restored, then sold again and is now painted maroon, named 'Loch Arkaig' and is hauling the Royal Scotsman train during 2005! *(Nick Meskell collection)*

Below: Among the great attractions of Scotland are the Class 37s and scenes like this. It's a cloudy dry day in the middle of summer but just over the roof of the loco, traces of snow can be seen in hidden crevices of the Cairngorm Mountains. 37 114 'Dunrobin Castle' is coupled to its train at Aviemore on 27th July 1986. For the record the other two 37s retained at Inverness for this train were 37 261 'Caithness' and 37 262 'Dounreay'. *(Nick Meskell collection)*

Above: The introduction of the Royal Scotsman brought with it the odd practice of stabling trains overnight at intermediate stations. As the train was (and still is) fully self contained, there was no need to de-train passengers. Eating, sleeping and entertainment were all provided within the nine coach formation, so why sit in a dull siding when you could stable on a long passing loop at a pretty station? Locations such as Keith (specific siding), Spean Bridge and Taynuilt (passing loops) offered the perfect surroundings and are still used today. Pictured at Taynuilt on 16th September 1989, 37 409 'Loch Awe' is bedded down for the night. On this particular day, passengers would have enjoyed steam-haulage from Fort William to Mallaig and back before 37 409 took them south to Crianlarich (run round) and with the evening meal being served, the final leg was the 29 mile, 100 minute journey to Taynuilt. In the morning, it was breakfast to Oban and then south. *(Nick Meskell collection)*

Opposite: This August 1988 shot shows 37 412 'Loch Lomond' arriving with the Royal Scotsman at Oban. Having stabled at Taynuilt overnight, it was a 13 mile, 35 minute run through to Oban before a 90 minute leg stretch/loco run round, then off south, probably to Edinburgh. 37 412 left Scotland in 1989 with a move to Laira and subsequently became 'Driver John Elliot' when based at Cardiff in the mid/late-1990s. At this time, the loco gained notoriety, often working the famous Fridays only 1M89, the 16.45 from Cardiff Central to Manchester Oxford Road, returning on 1V92, the 21.38 Crewe to Cardiff. *(Nick Meskell collection)*

Above: Towards the end of the 1980s, the carriages which worked the Royal Scotsman train were changed and with the new stock came a new livery. With 37 413 'Loch Eil Outward Bound' at the helm, this would appear to be the second or perhaps the third train, and was probably air braked. Heating probably wasn't required for the bulk of trains and neither was an ETS supply as the former BSK coach behind the loco had a diesel generator which provided power for the kitchen and internal lighting etc. The loco was there for its hauling power only. Taken on 13th October 1989, the train is pictured near Dundee. *(Nick Meskell collection)*

Below: Breaking the rule of blue locos only in this book, this gem of a shot of 37 356 was too good to omit. It shows that it wasn't always Eastfield or Inverness locos in charge - it's a Railfreight engine, renumbered and in a special pool and it wasn't even Scottish! Tinsley-based 37 356 'Grainflow' is pictured on 7th August 1988 at Carnoustie. Formerly 37 068, this loco had strong North East connections and was never based in Scotland. Renumbered in 1988 (for one year only), it was one of a number of unrefurbished Class 37/0s fitted with regeared bogies and was in the FGWB (Speedlink Distribution) pool at the time. What makes this photo even more delightful is that the train is on the wrong line due to engineering work and single line working on this particular Sunday! *(Nick Meskell collection)*

Loch Rannoch

37 408

Aluminium 100

37 410

Oor Wullie

37 402

Highland Region

37 417

The Scottish Hosteller

37 420

A DAY IN HISTORY - Friday 20th June 1986

Selected at random, here is a typical day from the summer of 1986 showing all known Class 37 passenger workings on the West Highland and Far North lines. It was an interesting period with both 37/0 and 37/4 operation. These are not the diagrams, this is what the locos actually worked. It also highlights that these locos didn't keep to their booked diagrams, an example being 37 410 which should have worked another Glasgow - Oban round trip but its place was taken by 37 188.

EASTFIELD LOCOS

37 188
1Y13 12.20 Glasgow QS to Oban
1T44 18.00 Oban to Glasgow QS

37 401
1Y21 09.50 Glasgow QS to Fort William
2Y55 16.05 Fort William to Mallaig
2Y58 18.50 Mallaig to Fort William
2Y57 21.05 Fort William to Mallaig

37 402
2Y52 06.50 Mallaig to Fort William
1T18 08.40 Fort William to Glasgow QS
1M16 22.35 Glasgow QS to Mossend

37 405
1Y51 10.05 Fort William to Mallaig
1Y54 12.20 Mallaig to Fort William
2Y53 14.05 Fort William to Mallaig
1T46 15.50 Mallaig to Fort William
1M16 17.40 Fort William to Glasgow QS

37 409
1Y23 16.50 Glasgow QS to Fort William

37 410
1T12 08.00 Oban to Glasgow QS

37 412
1S07 03.12 Mossend to Cowlairs
1S07 06.00 Glasgow QS to Fort William
1T34 14.15 Fort William to Glasgow QS

37 413
1Y11 08.20 Glasgow QS to Oban
1T28 13.00 Oban to Glasgow QS
1Y15 18.20 Glasgow QS to Oban

INVERNESS LOCOS

37 114
2H83 10.55 Inverness to Kyle
2H84 17.10 Kyle to Inverness

37 414
2H63 11.35 Inverness to Wick
2H64 18.00 Wick to Inverness

37 415
2H80 07.10 Kyle to Inverness

37 416
2H81 06.55 Inverness to Kyle
2H82 11.10 Kyle to Inverness
2H85 17.55 Inverness to Kyle

37 417
2H61 06.35 Inverness to Wick
2H62 12.00 Wick to Inverness

37 419
2H70 06.02 Thurso to Georgemas Jct
2H71 10.41 Georgemas Jct to Thurso
2H72 12.02 Thurso to Georgemas Jct
2H73 15.27 Georgemas Jct to Thurso
2H74 18.02 Thurso to Georgemas Jct
2H75 21.27 Georgemas Jct to Thurso

(Unknown)
2H60 06.00 Wick to Inverness
2H65 17.35 Inverness to Wick

The two above trains are unrecorded but, as a guess, 37 114 worked the 06.00 from Wick with either 37 415 or 37 417 working the 17.35 to Wick.

7D10

Since it features a number of times in the book, here is the booked path for 7D10, the 06.05 from Fort William to Mossend Yard, (shown as far as Craigendorran Junction).

Although just short of 100 miles in distance, the journey took over five hours with four stops to allow other trains to pass, one crew change and a prolonged period (50 minutes) at Tyndrum Upper. This would have been a typical path for a WHL freight train in the mid-1980s.

06.05	**depart Mallaig Junction Yard T.C.**
06.08	**arrive Mallaig Junction**
06.10	**depart Mallaig Junction**
06.30	**depart Spean Bridge**
06.50	**depart Tulloch**
07.34	**depart Rannoch**
08.00	**arrive Bridge of Orchy**
1S07	*passes heading to Fort William*
08.07	**depart Bridge of Orchy**
08.26	**arrive Tyndrum Upper**
7Y31	*passes heading to Fort William*
Crew change	
09.16	**depart Tyndrum Upper**
09.30	**depart Crianlarich**
09.54	**arrive Ardlui**
1Y11	*passes heading for Oban*
10.03	**depart Ardlui**
10.18	**depart Arrochar & Tarbet**
10.32	**depart Glen Douglas**
10.44	**arrive Garelochhead**
1Y21	*passes for Fort William*
10.50	**depart Garelochhead**
11.10	**depart Craigendoran Junction**

Information comes from the BR Working Timetable (Section GD) dated 11th May 1987 to 15th May 1988.

CRIANLARICH

Down Trains - Mondays to Saturdays - Summer 1987

The following table shows all Down trains which were due to pass or call at Crianlarich station in the summer of 1987. The information comes from the BR Working Timetable Section GD.

Headcode	Arrive	Depart	Days	Train
1S07	07.30	07.34	....	20.55 London Euston to Fort William
7Y31	....	08.08	SX	05.10 Mossend Yard to Fort William
7Y33	....	08.08	SO	05.10 Mossend Yard to Corpach Pulp Mill
1Y11	10.22	10.24	....	08.20 Glasgow Queen Street to Oban
1Y21	11.44	11.46	....	09.50 Glasgow Queen Street to Fort William
2Y91	....	12.35	TFSO	12.35 Crianlarich to Oban (DMU)
7Y39	....	13.11	MWFO	09.52 Mossend Yard to Oban
1Y13	14.14	14.16	....	12.20 Glasgow Queen Street to Oban
7Y37	15.30	15.38	SX	12.23 Mossend Yard to Corpach Pulp Mill
6S56	....	16.15	TO	07.12 Blyth Dock to Fort William
2Y93	....	16.19	TFSO	16.19 Crianlarich to Oban (DMU)
1Z98	....	17.26	TO	14.18 Edinburgh to Spean Bridge
6S56	....	17.28	TSX	07.12 Blyth Dock to Fort William
1Z98	16.58	17.35	WO	14.40 Fort William to Taynuilt
1Y23	18.44	18.46	....	16.50 Glasgow Queen Street to Fort William
1Y15	20.22	20.24	....	18.20 Glasgow Queen Street to Oban

Observation:
All trains were booked for Class 37s (singles or pairs) except the Crianlarich - Oban shuttle which was a DMU. 1S07 contained air con stock and was air braked. This train is described as 'Passenger and News from Euston'. All other passenger trains were vacuum braked. All freight trains were air braked although 6S56 could be vacuum braked when required. 6S56 is described as COY (Company Train). All other freight trains are SLK (Speedlink). 1Z98 is the Royal Scotsman. On Wednesdays the loco runs around the train at Crianlarich. 1Y23 has a bizarre stopping point on Thursdays. The text reads: 'Stops THO at Glen Douglas for domestic purposes and when required between Tyndrum and Bridge of Orchy'. To avoid confusion, the freight trains are shown to terminate at Fort William. The timetable shows them at Mallaig Junction Yard T.C. which is obviously in Fort William. Although off this table, 2Y55 which was the 16.10 from Fort William to Mallaig was booked for passenger and freight vehicles and is described as 'Mixed'.

Up Trains - Mondays to Saturdays - Summer 1987

The following table shows all Up trains which were due to pass or call at Crianlarich station in the summer of 1987. The information comes from the BR Working Timetable Section GD.

Headcode	Arrive	Depart	Days	Train
1T12	09.09	09.11	....	08.00 Oban to Glasgow Queen Street
7D10	....	09.30	....	06.05 Fort William to Mossend Yard
1T18	10.24	10.26	....	08.30 Fort William to Glasgow Queen Street
2Y96	11.18	....	TFSO	09.55 Oban to Crianlarich (DMU)
7D23	....	12.24	MWFO	09.30 Oban to Mossend Yard
1Z98	....	13.14	THO	10.35 Oban to Ladybank
1T28	14.09	14.15	....	13.00 Oban to Glasgow Queen Street
7D19	15.31	15.33	SX	12.23 Corpach Pulp Mill to Mossend Yard
2Y94	15.47	....	TFSO	14.35 Oban to Crianlarich (DMU)
1T34	16.08	16.10	TSX	14.15 Fort William to Glasgow Queen Street
1T34	16.08	16.16	TO	14.15 Fort William to Glasgow Queen Street
6E46	16.57	17.27	TO	14.25 Fort William to Mossend Yard
1Z98	16.58	17.35	WO	14.40 Fort William to Taynuilt
6E46	....	17.56	SX	15.19 Fort William to Mossend Yard
1T44	19.09	19.13	....	18.00 Oban to Glasgow Queen Street
1T46	19.40	19.42	SO	15.50 Mallaig to Glasgow Queen Street
1M16	19.40	19.42	SX	17.42 Fort William to London Euston

Observation:

All trains were booked for Class 37s (singles or pairs) except the Crianlarich - Oban shuttle which was a DMU. Although departing Oban 25 minutes earlier, on Fridays 7D23 was booked to recess at Taynuilt from 09.58 to 11.09 to allow 2Y96 to pass. 7D23 also had the letter 'Y' inserted, meaning 'Runs to and from Terminals/Yards as determined by traffic demand'. There are no times shown for 1T34 on Saturdays, although it definitely ran on Saturdays. It is assumed the TSX heading should read TX. 1M16 contained air con stock and was air braked. All other passenger trains were vacuum braked. All freight trains were air braked although 6E46 could be vacuum braked when required. 6E56 is described as COY (Company Train) and although shown to terminate at Mossend, with an 'E' headcode, the train would add/detach wagons at this location before continuing to Blyth Dock. All other freight trains were SLK (Speedlink). 1Z98 is the Royal Scotsman. On Wednesdays the loco ran around the train at Crianlarich. Similar to 1Y23 on the down line, 1T18 had an unusual stopping point on Thursdays. The text reads: 'Stops THO when required for domestic purposes at 44.5 mile post between Bridge of Orchy and Tyndrum Upper'. To avoid confusion, the freight trains are shown to start at Fort William. The timetable shows them at Mallaig Junction Yard T.C. which is obviously in Fort William. Although off this table, 2Y58 which was the 18.50 from Mallaig to Fort William was booked for passenger and freight vehicles and is described as 'Mixed'. 2T46 which was the 15.50 from Mallaig to Fort William (SX) has the words 'Conveys Glasgow Portion' in the column.

Still Available

SCOTTISH CLASS 37s
Volume One
This book covers the 1980-1986 period featuring Class 37/0s based at Inverness and Eastfield. It's all steam heat, mostly BR blue or early large logo with Mark 1 coaches and vacuum braked freights.

52 pages - £9.95

CLASS 56 PICTORIAL
This book takes a look at the Class 56 locomotive. From the early days in BR blue through the multicoloured 1980s and 1990s, right through to the EWS years, more than 50 different locos are featured. This book is a timely reminder of what really was a classic of loco classes - The Class 56.

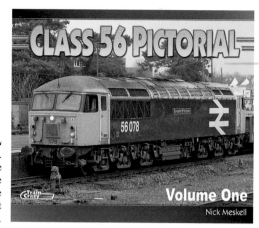

60 pages - £9.95

Coming Soon

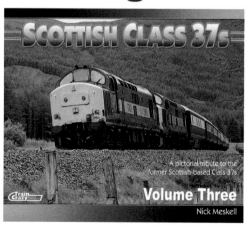

SCOTTISH CLASS 37s
Volume Three
The third and final book in this series concludes the Class 37 story in Scotland. From the late 1980s through to the present day, follow the story of the Eastfield, Motherwell and Inverness locos through the days of pre-privatisation to the EWS years. Lots of different liveries are shown including Inter City, Civil Engineers, Regional Railways and Royal Scotsman. As the 37/4s went south, 37/0s returned on passenger trains and old favourites like 37 025 returned to the Highlands!

Release date: To be announced. (See our website and adverts in the railway press for more details)

CLASS 37s IN SCOTLAND
DVD AND VIDEO
You've read the book - now see the movie!

This special programme looks at Class 37s and other diesels in Scotland in the 1980s. Many of the locos pictured in this book are featured including 37/0s in blue and large logo and the 37/4s working passenger and freight trains, summer and winter.

The perfect companion to this book series.

Release date: October 2005 (See our website and adverts in the railway press for more details)

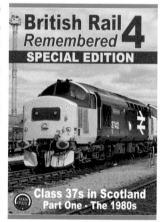

For full details of all these titles, please contact us or visit our website:

www.train-crazy.co.uk
Many other titles available.

Please contact us for full details of all of these items and a copy of our free catalogue.

Post: Train Crazy, FREEPOST, Blackpool. FY4 1BR.
Telephone & Fax: 01253 346005
email: admin@train-crazy.co.uk
website: www.train-crazy.co.uk